## **General Background**

In November of 2017, I began at an Amazon fulfillment center in West Columbia, SC known as CAE1. Prior to working there, I had no idea that a place I often online shopped from was fulfilling some of my orders just seven miles away from my residence. Although I did not immediately get the hang of things there, eventually I did and soon skyrocketed towards success within the company.

Prior to Amazon and during my attendance at the University of South Carolina, I have held numerous leadership positions including:

Expeditor/shift leader at Buffalo Wild Wings
Orientation Leader at the University of South Carolina
Coach/trainer for Integrity Staffing Solutions
Process Guide for Pack Department at Amazon
Engagement Process Assistant for Stow and Pick Departments at Amazon

    I recently graduated from the Darla Moore School of Business at the University of South Carolina with honors and leadership distinction. All of these positions have in some way, shape or form opened my eyes to various leadership styles. "What is a leader?" This is a question I pondered for many years because I was not always led by the most effective management team. After numerous observations and experiences, I am able to have a better understanding of what leadership practices cultivate the most positive results. And in this book, I share those essential principles with you. I hope you enjoy and grasp key takeaways!

What is effective management? More specifically, what is effective management from the perspective of an employee? Consider this: most books or articles about management are written by one of three people:

Managers who have experience managing
Graduates who possess a management-related degree
Criticizer of management (i.e. a disgruntled employee)

However, rarely (very rarely) are books or articles about management written by an employee who is not disgruntled and who has carefully examined ways in which certain management styles have been either effective or ineffective with their team of employees.

## **Examination of Amazon's Leadership Principles**

Examining Amazon's fourteen leadership principles explicitly from the perspective of manager to associate allows us to understand them from not an *associate to customer* standpoint but just as equally important, a *manager to associate* viewpoint. Because ultimately, managers are here to serve those in which they lead.

1. **Customer Obsession**

    Leaders start with the customer and work backwards. They work vigorously to earn and keep customer trust. Although leaders pay attention to competitors, they obsess over customers.

*Managers must think of their employees as their customers with respect to servant leadership. Keeping their employees satisfied consequently makes them satisfy the customers of the company – the consumers.*

2. **Ownership**

> Leaders are owners. They think long term and don't sacrifice long-term value for short-term results. They act on behalf of the entire company, beyond just their own team. They never say, "that's not my job."

*As an owner, managers must act when something goes wrong and when decisions need to be made. They do not shy away from getting their hands dirty and tackling tasks that are outside of their regularly scheduled program (i.e. less overseeing, more hands on).*

3. **Invent and Simplify**

   Leaders expect and require innovation and invention from their teams and always find ways to simplify. They are externally aware, look for new ideas from everywhere, and are not limited by "not invented here". Because we do new things, we accept that we may be misunderstood for long periods of time.

   *It is imperative that as a manager, you are open to*

*changes suggested by your team of associates. If not, associates become complacent and discontent because they feel as though their ideas are baseless and unrecognized.*

4. **Are Right, A Lot**

   Leaders are right a lot. They have strong judgement and good instincts. They seek diverse perspectives and work to disconfirm their beliefs.
*Managers are leaders but so are their associates. Be open to various perspectives as a manager because your perspective is not always solid.*

*As a manager, you are not over a team but instead are a part of it; accepting different beliefs creates camaraderie and diversity.*

## 5. **Learn and Be Curious**

Leaders are never done learning and always seek to improve themselves. They are curious about new possibilities and act to explore them.

*Take the time as a manager to learn the "tick" to the "tock" of your team. Improvement in your associates is a direct reflection of improvement within you.*

## 6. **Hire and Develop the Best**

Leaders raise the performance bar with every hire and promotion. They recognize people with exceptional talent and willingly move them throughout the organization. Leaders develop leaders and are serious about their role in coaching others. We work on behalf of our people to invent mechanisms for development like Career Choice.

*The best coaches are those who can seamlessly connect with their team members on a one on one basis. By learning the strengths and weaknesses of each associate, a manager can better assist with structuring this individual in a way that will exploit their talents (those beneficial to the company).*

## 7. Insist on the Highest Standards

Leaders have relentlessly high standards – many people may think these standards are unreasonably high. Leaders are continually raising the bar and driving their teams to deliver high quality products, services and processes. Leaders ensure that defects do not get sent down the line and that problems are fixed so they stay fixed.

*Your team of associates are your front-line. Keep this in mind. Their energy is literally derived from you as the manager. Set the benchmark bar high while actively realizing that they are humans – not numbers.*

8. **Think Big**

Thinking small is a self-fulfilling prophecy. Leaders create and communicate a bold direction that inspires results. They think differently and look around corners for ways to serve customers.

*Be open to new ideas presented by your team of associates. Create an atmosphere that promotes outside of the box thinking.*

## 9. **Bias for Action**

Speed matters in business. Many decisions and actions are reversible and do not need extensive study. We value calculated risk taking.

*It is not apparent why associates perform their tasks the way that they do sometimes; what is most important, however, is that as long as it is within the rules and regulations, allow them to complete tasks in a manner that best suits their means.*

10. **Frugality**

Accomplish more with less. Constraints breed resourcefulness, self-sufficiency and invention. There are no extra points for growing headcount, budget size or fixed expense. *This is tricky from manager to associate standpoint because you do not want to make the associate feel like a "number" or "disposable." Business needs are business needs and sometimes these needs are unfavorable for the associate. During times like this, it is imperative that the associate is greatly appreciated for any and all contributions they have made.*

## 11. Earn Trust

Leaders listen attentively, speak candidly, and treat others respectfully. They are vocally self-critical, even when doing so is awkward or embarrassing. Leaders do not believe their or their team's body odor smells of perfume. They benchmark themselves and their teams against the best.

*Managers are already faced with the belief that associates feel inferior to them. To combat this, actively engage with your associates by not only interacting with them when there is an issue, but also when everything is smooth sailing. And most importantly, uphold all promises; nothing puts a bigger dent in trust than being let down. Ultimately, you want the "buy in" of your team members because without that, they're highly unlikely to "go the distance" for positive results.*

## 12. Dive Deep

Leaders operate at all levels, stay connected to the details, audit frequently, and are skeptical when metrics and anecdote differ. No task is beneath them.

*Partner with your team of associates about potential barriers they are encountering. This alleviates downstream issues and deepens your connection with members of the team.*

## 13. Have Backbone; Disagree and Commit

Leaders are obligated to respectfully challenge decisions when they disagree, even when doing so is uncomfortable or exhausting. Leaders have conviction and are tenacious. They do not compromise for the sake of social cohesion. Once a decision is determined, they commit wholly.

*Sometimes, managers and associates are going to agree to disagree. Do not expect your associates to compromise their feelings towards something because you are not on the same page as them. Expect feedback that differs from yours. Be open to various perspectives so long as they are presented in a respectful manner.*

## 14. **Deliver Results**

Leaders focus on the key inputs for their business and deliver them with the right quality and in a timely fashion. Despite setbacks, they rise to the occasion and never compromise.

*Motivate, motivate, motivate. Any manager who possesses that uplifting and energetic spirit is on the right track to ensuring that their team delivers the best results. When it is time to deliver (negative or positive) results to a member of your team, keep in mind that your approach is the ultimate determinant of change or consistency. Remember to attack the process, engage the people (APEP). Results are easily delivered when barriers of the associate are removed.*

## **Nine Effective Management Principles by CK**

Employees of the company are, in a sense, potential future leaders. So, it is important to now "dive deeper" into specific qualities that managers should possess in order to have a receptive, capable (and willing) and eager team of associates.

I have personally developed nine effective management principles. Why nine when there could be many, many more? Nine symbolizes divine completeness or conveys the meaning of totality. With these nine principles, I am hoping that managers can get a grapple on or an idea of what will make their team churn out unbelievably amazing results. It imperative that managers are customer-centric in regard to the associate. Through writing this, I am also hoping that employees will be able to better communicate the form of guidance that they need from their management team. Those nine principles are outlined as followed:

1. Acknowledge That It Is a Team, Not Just Management

The "lowest person" on totem pole is a direct reflection of the "highest person" on it. This means that managers must realize and accept their dependence on their employees because without them, the success of the operations is highly unlikely. For example: if a manager solely takes credit for meeting the department's goals for the evening, this is likely to depreciate the motivation of their employees to achieve continued success because no one is a fan of being unrecognized for their efforts. Instill and constantly re-instill within your team that without them, you are extremely limited in achievability. Boosting overall morale is the main objective (always keep this in mind).

2. Avoid Being Passive Aggressive

Being indirect often fosters resistance in their employees whether managers realize this or not. I have witnessed and been a victim of passive aggression within the workplace. I can assure you that it feels belittling and downright disrespectful. Why? Because it makes the employee develop the mindset of spite. Essentially, they begin to think "since you can't be direct, I am not going to go above and beyond for you." Now, as a manager, you receive the bare minimum (if that). For example:

managers have rules that they must make sure that their employees adhere to; at Amazon, one of those rules are hair above the shoulders. This ensures the safety of the employee because there are numerous conveyor belts within the warehouse. As a manager, you discover that one associate does not have their hair above their shoulders every now and again, but the other employees adhere to this rule. Instead of addressing this specific employee, you (as the manager) feel the need to get on the microphone as this associate passes you by and give a publicized reminder to all associates. You have now done two things as a manager: embarrassed the associate who does not have his or her hair above their shoulders and made associates who are close to the embarrassed associate now have disdain for you. A lot of managers would not care about this newfound reality. However, those will be the same managers who struggle to realize that it is now the cause of poor performance amongst some of their associates. Associates are cliquish and disdain for you as a manager can spread rapidly. How can this be avoided? Interact one on one with the associate about any violations observed. This ties directly into the next principle of effective management.

3. Build Connections on a 1:1 Ratio

Nothing is more personal to an associate (work-wise) than a fostered one on one connection with their manager or management team. This boosts employee morale and consequently, their willingness to meet the needs of the company. There is something refreshing about seeing your manager walk towards you and you don't immediately assume that you've done something terrible. Instead, they are approaching you just to pry into how life is treating you. And for a manager, if the associate has done something inappropriate or unsatisfactory, having this previously established connection makes the engagement not only more positive despite its negative topic, but more effective and likely to lead to an improvement. This involves finding a balance between empathizing and remaining work-oriented. For example: you have an associate who underperformed last week, but normally does well and you have highlighted their achievements on a continual basis. This corrective interaction about their dip in performance is now highly likely to result in a reversion to an improved performance. Why? Because the manager didn't solely interact with the associate when things seemed to have been falling apart for him or her, but instead, also congratulated the associate when their work ethic was astounding. Who knows, the manager could have also gotten close enough to the associate to know that certain, unpleasant factors unrelated to work may have caused this dip in performance. It is not always about crunching the numbers because at the end of the day, every member of your team is human and should be regarded as such.

4. Be Mindful of Body Language

Since I was a wee little thing, I was taught that often times, our bodies speak before our mouths have the ability to speak. Obviously, there was some truth to this belief because I was constantly reprimanded by my mother for "negative body language." The same could be true about managers because it is often unbeknownst to us due to our body expressions becoming our personal commonplace. Associates feed off of the energy of their manager. If their manager is upbeat, it has a tendency to flow into the associates as well.

One evening at my first Amazon site, as a Seasonal Engagement PA, I was not feeling too excited for yet another overnight shift. However, once my manager at the time greeted me with the most upbeat energy (even asked about my day), it changed my entire picture of the night ahead.

It is not always that simple. But I can assure you if management appears miserable, the associate is highly unlikely to have a positive attitude when it comes to their task(s). I have experienced times when I did not want to be at work and it was evident that my manager was not happy to be there either; the negative energy of my manager, consequently, extended to the rest of the team and this caused a decline in performance and benchmark rates.

5. Sidestep the Abuse of Authoritative Antics

No one appreciates managers who have to constantly remind themselves of their authoritative powers. Your team does not need a reminder that you are their leader; this was established at the first assembly. Managers do not understand how that makes their team less productive, less proficient and less receptible to change. There is already an inferiority complex that is present (associate versus manager); do not exploit this but rather disregard its existence. This can be achieved by jumping in and providing hands-on assistance when tasks become too cumbersome. And when things are flowing smoothly, still "get your hands dirty" as a manager because this demonstrates that you are not above your team, but instead are a part of it.

## 6. Regulate and Minimize Delegation

One of the worst character traits that can be given to a manger is *lazy*. As managers, you are definitely going to have multiple things to juggle at once. However, this does not mean free up your hands just to fill the hands of your associates. Demanding too much can lead to associates feeling demeaned; this consequently dampens your credibility as a servant leader.

Delegation is intertwined into the personality type of an individual. A person who possesses a "Type A" personality, generally does not delegate much because they believe it is best done if done by themselves.

- Pros: More reliable, motivated, punctual and efficient
- Cons: More hostile, impatient and competitive

Those who have a "Type B" personality, however, find it more difficult to complete tasks themselves.

- Pros: Experimental, reflective and relaxed
- Cons: procrastinator, uncommitted and passive

I would consider myself to have a Type A personality, and I can certainly be described as an impatient go-getter. In interviews, I describe my weaknesses in two words – delegation and perfection. It is hard to find a delicate balance between trusting those around you to get the job done and inserting yourself to make sure the job gets done. As a manager, however, it is important to find this balance because too much delegation makes you look lazy and not enough delegation makes your team feel as if they are untrustworthy. Try to assign tasks on the basis of duration and the skillset required to complete them. This involves leaning into the associate's strengths more so than their weaknesses.

7. Prevent Favoritism

As humans, we naturally gravitate towards people who are compatible to us. Yes, I said compatible, so feel free to challenge me on the ole "opposites attract" cliché. In terms of management, managers like employees who embody work ethic beliefs similar to theirs. That is perfectly fine. However, it becomes imperfect when this associate begins to receive special treatment due to the mere fact that they are a "manager's pet." If another associate is late from break and you chose to write him or her up, the same needs to happen for the "manager pet" or a division is created. This division leads to broken policy and a broken policy clearly reflects that inconsistency and unfairness is prevalent. It also poisons the morale of your team and heightens tensions.

## 8. Incentivize Employees

Remember as a five-year-old when you were rewarded for completing small tasks such as placing your toys in a chest or eating your veggies? That same joy felt at the tender age of five, is the same rush of happiness that comes over an employee when a manger notices their strides. As humans, we like to be rewarded for our achievements. Several managers have a simple thought process – "why should I reward an associate for doing their job?" However, by thinking that, how are you making this associate want to even continue doing their job so well? Remember, they make you (the manager) look good by performing well – not vice versa. It is beneficial to managers to commend associates one on one and reward them with company incentives such as extended breaks and lunches. A correlation can almost always be seen between production and feedback form associates.

9. Actively Trust Your Team

As managers, you're not always right nor are your ideas always the holy grail. It is imperative that managers express or convey a sense of trust in their team. This can come across in a variety of ways. For example, listen to their ideas and help them develop creative avenues to place these abstract ideas into concrete settings. At Amazon, you cannot find a better setting to achieve this. The company is rapidly expanding and innovating. In the leadership principles, "Invent and Simply" and "Think Big" are two key principles that connect to this. Your associates are on the front line of whatever process path they are in; with that being noted, does it not make sense to trust their suggestions for improvement being that they have the greatest exposure in that particular area? Mangers must go from a paternalistic approach to an individualized approach to achieve customer satisfaction. Again, there is already an inferiority complex that is present (associate versus manager); do not exploit this but rather disregard its existence. Trust their suggestions because they trust your process. This rapport could prove beneficial down the line when you need an associate to stick their neck out on the line for you. It also reduces what is known as the credibility gap – an apparent difference between what is said or promised and what happens or is true.

## **Succinct Conclusion**

It is important to note that there is no such thing as a "perfect manager." However, it is possible for an understanding, collaborative and engaging manager to exist. One that acknowledges each associate as an individual who deserves development and consistency.

# **Notes**

www.ingramcontent.com/pod-product-compliance
Lightning Source LLC
Chambersburg PA
CBHW051204170526
45158CB00005B/1814